People in My Community/La gente de mi comunidad

Sanitation Worker/ El recogedor de basura

JoAnn Early Macken
photographs by/fotografías de Gregg Andersen

Reading consultant/Consultora de lectura: Susan Nations, M.Ed., author/literacy coach/consultant

WEEKLY (WR) READER®
EARLY LEARNING LIBRARY

Please visit our web site at: **www.earlyliteracy.cc**
For a free color catalog describing Weekly Reader® Early Learning Library's
list of high-quality books, call 1-877-445-5824 (USA) or 1-800-387-3178 (Canada).
Weekly Reader® Early Learning Library's fax: (414) 336-0164.

Library of Congress Cataloging-in-Publication Data

Macken, JoAnn Early, 1953-
    [Sanitation worker. Spanish & English]
    Sanitation worker = El recogedor de basura
        p. cm. — (People in my community = La gente de mi comunidad)
    Summary: Photographs and simple text describe the work done by sanitation workers.
    Includes bibliographical references and index.
    ISBN 0-8368-3674-X (lib. bdg.)
    ISBN 0-8368-3688-X (softcover)
    1. Sanitation workers—Juvenile literature. 2. Refuse and refuse disposal—Juvenile literature.
    [1. Sanitation workers. 2. Occupations. 3. Spanish language materials—Bilingual.]
    I. Title: Recogedor de basura. II. Title. III. People in my community. Spanish & English.
    HD8039.S257M3318   2003
    628.4'42—dc21   2002044925

Updated and reprinted in 2005.
First published in 2003 by
Weekly Reader® Early Learning Library
330 West Olive Street, Suite 100
Milwaukee, WI 53212 USA

Copyright © 2003 by Weekly Reader® Early Learning Library

Art direction: Tammy Gruenewald
Page layout: Katherine A. Goedheer
Photographer: Gregg Andersen
Editorial assistant: Diane Laska-Swanke
Translators: Colleen Coffey and Consuelo Carrillo

Printed in the United States of America

2 3 4 5 6 7 8 9 09 08 07 06 05

Note to Educators and Parents

Reading is such an exciting adventure for young children! They are beginning to integrate their oral language skills with written language. To encourage children along the path to early literacy, books must be colorful, engaging, and interesting; they should invite the young reader to explore both the print and the pictures.

People in My Community is a new series designed to help children read about the world around them. In each book young readers will learn interesting facts about some familiar community helpers.

Each book is specially designed to support the young reader in the reading process. The familiar topics are appealing to young children and invite them to read — and re-read — again and again. The full-color photographs and enhanced text further support the student during the reading process.

In addition to serving as wonderful picture books in schools, libraries, homes, and other places where children learn to love reading, these books are specifically intended to be read within an instructional guided reading group. This small group setting allows beginning readers to work with a fluent adult model as they make meaning from the text. After children develop fluency with the text and content, the book can be read independently. Children and adults alike will find these books supportive, engaging, and fun!

Una nota a los educadores y a los padres

¡La lectura es una emocionante aventura para los niños! En esta etapa están comenzando a integrar su manejo del lenguaje oral con el lenguaje escrito. Para fomentar la lectura desde una temprana edad, los libros deben ser vistosos, atractivos e interesantes; deben invitar al joven lector a explorar tanto el texto como las ilustraciones.

La gente de mi comunidad es una nueva serie pensada para ayudar a los niños a conocer el mundo que los rodea. En cada libro, los jóvenes lectores conocerán datos interesantes sobre el trabajo de distintas personas de la comunidad.

Cada libro ha sido especialmente diseñado para facilitar el proceso de lectura. La familiaridad con los temas tratados atrae la atención de los niños y los invita a leer — y releer — una y otra vez. Las fotografías a todo color y el tipo de letra facilitan aún más al estudiante el proceso de lectura.

Además de servir como fantásticos libros ilustrados en la escuela, la biblioteca, el hogar y otros lugares donde los niños aprenden a amar la lectura, estos libros han sido concebidos específicamente para ser leídos en grupos de instrucción guiada. Este contexto de grupos pequeños permite que los niños que se inician en la lectura trabajen con un adulto cuya fluidez les sirve de modelo para comprender el texto. Una vez que se han familiarizado con el texto y el contenido, los niños pueden leer los libros por su cuenta. ¡Tanto niños como adultos encontrarán que estos libros son útiles, entretenidos y divertidos!

— Susan Nations, M.Ed., author, literacy coach,
and consultant in literacy development

Sanitation workers help keep a community clean. They pick up garbage and recyclables.

- - - - - - -

Los recogedores de basura ayudan a mantener la comunidad limpia. Ellos recogen la basura y cosas reciclables.

Sanitation workers carry heavy garbage cans. They lift heavy bags into a truck.

- - - - - - - -

Los recogedores de basura cargan botes de basura muy pesados. Ponen bolsas de basura en un camión grande.

Sanitation workers wear gloves. Gloves help them get a good grip. Gloves protect their hands from sharp objects, dirt, and germs.

■ ■ ■ ■ ■ ■ ■

Los recogedores de basura llevan guantes. Estos guantes los ayudan a agarrar bien los botes. También protegen las manos de objetos afilados, suciedad y bacteria.

9

Sanitation workers drive big **garbage trucks**. They usually drive a different route each day of the week.

Ellos manejan **camiones de la basura**. Estos camiones son grandes y van por una ruta diferente cada día de la semana.

garbage truck/
camión de la basura

At the end of the day,
they empty the truck.
The garbage goes into a
landfill or an incinerator.

＿ ＿ ＿ ＿ ＿ ＿ ＿

Al final del día, vacían el
camión. Llevan la basura a
una planta procesadora de
residuos o a un incinerador.

Sanitation workers also drive
street sweepers. The street
sweepers pick up leaves and
spray water on the streets
to clean them.

— — — — — — — —

Los recogedores de basura
manejan barredoras también.
Las barredoras recogen las
hojas y echan agua en las
calles para limpiarlas.

Sanitation workers collect trash from parks. They pick up litter from streets and sidewalks.

- - - - - - - -

Los recogedores de basura recogen basura de los parques. También la recogen de las calles y las aceras.

They work in any kind of weather. Where it snows, they may drive **snowplows** in the winter.

– – – – – – – –

Ellos trabajan en toda clase de tiempo. En invierno manejan **palas para quitar la nieve** en los lugares donde hay nieve.

snowplow/palas
para quitar la nieve

Trash belongs in a **trash can**. You don't litter, do you?

– – – – – – – –

La basura se debe poner en un **basurero**. Tú no la tiras fuera de su lugar, ¿verdad?

trash can/basurero

21

Glossary/Glosario

incinerator — a furnace or container for burning garbage

incinerador — aparato para quemar basura

landfill — a place where garbage is buried between layers of dirt

planta procesadora de residuos — lugar donde se entierra la basura

recyclables — objects like glass, plastic, and metal containers that can be treated or remade and used again.

reciclables — objetos de vidrio, plástico, y metal que se procesan y se vuelven a usar

route — a line of travel

ruta — camino

For More Information/Más información

Fiction Books/Libros de ficción

Rockwell, Anne F. *Career Day.*
   New York: HarperCollins Publishers, 2000.

Nonfiction Books/Libros de no ficción

Bourgeois, Paulette. *Garbage Collectors.*
   Buffalo: Kids Can Press, 1998.
Deedrick, Tami. *Garbage Collectors.* Mankato,
   Minn.: Bridgestone Books, 1998.
Johnson, Jean. *Sanitation Workers, A to Z.*
   New York: Walker, 1988.
Maynard, Christopher. *Jobs People Do.*
   New York: DK Publishing, 2001.

Web Sites/Páginas Web

What happens to your trash once you toss it?
www.kdhe.state.ks.us/kdsi/main_pg11.html
Waste management facts and resources from the Kansas
Department of Health and Environment

Index/Índice

About the Author/Información sobre la autora

JoAnn Early Macken is the author of children's poetry, two rhyming picture books, *Cats on Judy* and *Sing-Along Song* and various other nonfiction series. She teaches children to write poetry and received the Barbara Juster Esbensen 2000 Poetry Teaching Award. JoAnn is a graduate of the MFA in Writing for Children Program at Vermont College. She lives in Wisconsin with her husband and their two sons.

JoAnn Early Macken es autora de poesía para niños. Ha escrito dos libros de rimas con ilustraciones, *Cats on Judy* y *Sing-Along Song* y otras series de libros educativos para niños. Ella enseña a los niños a escribir poesía y ha ganado el Premio Barbara Juster Esbensen en el año 2000. JoAnn se graduó con el título de "MFA" en el programa de escritura infantil de Vermont College. Vive en Wisconsin con su esposo y sus dos hijos.